POETRY

POETRY
*UEA Postgraduate
Creative Writing Anthology
2017*

CONTENTS

PAUL MILLS *Foreword*   VII
SOPHIE ROBINSON *Introduction*   IX

DARIO BIAGINI	2
FERN BROOME RICHARDS	10
PAUL FREDERIK CARLSEN	14
DAVID CHARLES GILL	24
RICH LAW	34
NAOMI MADLOCK	40
S.Z. MASON	50
MOLLY ELLEN PEARSON	54
JAKE REYNOLDS	60
OLIVIA WALWYN	68
ARRON WESTBROOK	76
E.F. WILLIS	82

PAUL MILLS
Foreword

Reading these poems, I gradually became aware of a contradiction – one which I feel makes this anthology not just interesting on first reading but well worth returning to. On the one hand, I had a sense of experiencing new art, the page as art-space, poems as installations. This kind of practice has nothing to do with art appreciation, art as rhetoric, as in ekphrastic poems – making an explicit show of already known works and worlds of art – but offers something more radical. The look of a poem, its visual structure, features prominently in the work of each of the poets. Stanzas occur in dislodged alignments. Changes of font size, use of parenthesis, graphics, multiple slashes, typographical gaps, suggest architecture and imply a preference for deliberate design. And yet, on the other hand, repeatedly the content of this architecture (what happens, as it were, within its walls) carries a strong impression of spontaneity. What we hear is the very impulse of thinking, with surprising leaps, as if we are present during the act of composition itself, happening as it happens. Whether that actually is the case, I doubt. But in so many of the poems collected here, looking, thinking, making leaps, losing perspective, gaining it, being alert to distances between points, to maps, to place names, to mark-making, to how things connect and disconnect, is all part of the ready and available matter and register that generates the actual word-by-word content.

It seems inevitable therefore that the poems will be structures, and seen as such, given that structure and structuring make up so much of our experience and even create it. It follows too that they make themselves extra-alert to chance, to contingency, the antagonists of design, finding beauty, if at all, where nobody else has bothered to look. Awareness of structure (its dominance, limitations, ironies and doubts) becomes a kind of sensibility, with values. As voices too, they inhabit spaces of multiple, strange, non-coercive, interactive attention. And finally, in keeping with that, is the very obvious range, the lack of prescribed attitude – qualities this anthology has in abundance.

Paul Mills
Former Fellow of Creative Writing at the Universities of Leeds, Manchester and York, published by Carcanet and Smith Doorstop.

SOPHIE ROBINSON
Introduction

This is my fourth year teaching on the MA at UEA, and I am always both inspired and astounded by the range and breadth of talent each year's intake brings to the poetry workshop. This year has been no exception, as you're about to see.

Within the pages of this anthology are twelve distinctive, original and exciting poets, working in a range of disciplines and traditions, from the meditative pastoral lyric to the intense confessional to the conceptual and experimental. What has really struck me about working with this group is the ways in which they have approached each other's work on its own terms, allowing each of their peers to develop their practice along its own trajectory.

Dario Biagini's poems are full of knowing, winking humour and bilingual wordplay, exploring, with a tongue in its cheek, the complexities of an identity as it migrates between languages and countries: 'I need you to know my miniature Mussolini'.

Humour is also present in Fern Broome Richards's work, in the form of subtly absurd, small nouns like objects cutting across the otherwise sincere lyric evocations of feeling: 'the pork pie / split on its seams like a wounded heart'.

Paul Carlsen shares with Richards the ability to find profundity and depth of feeling in the everyday, in toothpaste left open to crust over by a lover. The tenderness of expression in Carlsen's poems is grounded by his use of dating, which both grounds us in a dailiness and also points to the necessary temporariness of these feelings, no matter how deeply felt they are in the moment of the poem.

In contrast, David Charles Gill's work balances expressions of tenderness and intimacy with exciting experiments in form and style, planting the personal and present within the ancient forest of lyric and dramatic tradition. I'm struck by Gill's skilful balance between articulating universal and timeless sentiments, and doing so in a way which feels at once wholly original and brand new, for example the powerful ending of 'Shit keeps getting everywhere': 'staying like a crumpled child who / can't be left and cannot bear to leave'.

Rich Law's work skilfully and playfully adopts multiple voices in a series of vivid snapshots, with a disarming clarity and preciseness. Law plays with our shared understanding of cultural iconography and archetypes at the same time as shining a new light on the detail and complexity of these characters through original, striking imagery, for example the meerkat with its 'paws / tableclothed over [its] / tummy'.

The vividness of S. Z. Mason's conceptual work comes from his precise, almost painterly use of the page, and his exploitation of poetry's communication through the visual and sonic qualities of language, shot through with beautiful and precise images: 'the sun overcoding the stars'.

Naomi Madlock's work has a distinctive, confident and meditative quality, and an impressive, close attentiveness to the small beauty found in each living moment, 'learn[ing] to listen / to the percolation of time'.

Olivia Walwyn's work also has a meditative lyric quality to it, each poem enchanting a reader through its sheer attentiveness to what is, and the speaker's astonishment at the small wonders of nature happening in the moment around: 'River held in the cliffbank / oh, and water gargling like it was / cupped to someone's mouth'.

Molly Ellen Pearson engages thoughtfully with the confessional tradition. The poems are engaging, intimate and frank, productively fragmented and disrupted through the use of experimental techniques and unexpected, moving and original imagery: 'as if the house of my face could / burn down with too much desire'.

Jake Reynolds also plays with the relationship between intimacy of address and formal experimentation, balancing this intimacy and immediacy with the largest questions of life. 'Frozen Aisle' is an excellent example of this, where Reynolds takes us on a meditative journey from the 'weird nuggets and chunks' of the supermarket to the 'stars, ringed planets, and other cold things of the universe'.

Arron Westbrook also expertly navigates the relationship between the private and public through the spectre of consumerism 'a shop soiled french stick / stolen from Tesco / snapped in half / i stitched back together / with the brightest red thread'. These lyric interjections into the flattened out landscape of capitalism have the effect of creating a highly charged politicised 'i', the speaker's thoughts and actions running like a red thread through the beige canvas of public life.

Similarly, E. F. Willis's work takes us from the specificities of the here-and-now to the larger questions of life through sheer attentiveness and close observation of the quiet moments of life, where the medical waiting room of 'Rheumatology' becomes a place in which 'light is spun out between breaths'.

It has been a pleasure to watch these students grow in talent and confidence, and a privilege to spend time with their work, both in workshops and through writing this introduction. From each student, I learnt something new about what a poem can do, and I can't wait to see what they do next.

Dr Sophie Robinson
Lecturer in Creative Writing at The University of East Anglia, published by Bloodaxe.

This diverse anthology comprises the latest work from the 2017 cohort of poets studying UEA's renowned Creative Writing MA.

DARIO BIAGINI

Dario Biagini is a part-time farmer based in Modena, Italy. He studied translation but this did not help with his accent. He generally writes about what he sees and what he eats. Most of all, he tries not to be boring.

Frontiersman

Please don't let me write another poem
on asparagus
Felix Pedro from my mountains
cut shoes out of bear's feet
Sasquatch footprints were found
near Fairbanks, Alaska
next to his golden creek

Don't let me save earth with a Prius
I read Fernanda on Papa's new refuge
in Cuba, and his latest
big catch. One more daiquiri now;
a bred trout doesn't count, *Santiago*

All I'm left with are your artificial enemies
bacteria fought with cannons
give me something less, a fair fight,
give me a poncho and a fistful
of dollars

Maps

Life off the motorway,
not for many.
For, to be off the route
far from the gathering crux
of human industriousness
you needn't be scared of solitude.
The shortest distance between two points
being a straight line,
many do not see the purpose
of a steering wheel.

Translation of a Northern Italian Dialect

Quand a s'era putlet
dimondi volti a' ndeeva a ca
d'i noon,
parché la mama l'era a
scoola a lavurer.
Me noona la feva l'ort e la maseva al galeini.
Al metod l'era un pooc brusc,
difati ghi tireva al col
Ah, quanti ori a vedr la noona fer la sfoja
pri caplèt !
Quanti fèti 'd parsut !
Per Nadel, a 's feva na tavleda
con tut i pareint. A s'era al più cic,
i'm vliven baser tut.
Cum l'era bela la fèta ad cudghein
vederla sblisgher in dal piàt ! E cum'i eren
boni al pan ad nadel e i tutlein frìt !
Ma anca adesa la va a basta bein,
anca s'i vech ini andedi tut. Ch'i eter
tinen a bota, anca me, c'a sun in mez
ai furaster.
A 'sfa sempr'in teimp a turner a cà
e per Nadel a magner e bever
n'eter bicher ad
Lambrosch.

In kindergarten at lunchtime
we received our weekly treat of
ice cream from ladies in hairnets,
normally living in the kitchen,
commonly referred to as the witch's
hut.
The single cup was sealed by a
printed cardboard lid portraying
a football.
The dessert consisted of two half cylinders
one chocolate, one vanilla.
Here things get interesting: the mainstream
tasting theory was rather hedonistic
chocolate being far superior
was the first half to go.
But at the time I hated chocolate.
I don't know if I should blame my
education or my temper, but I
insisted in consuming it first anyway,
to prove how stoic I was and to pay
homage to my coveted vanilla. The
result was the unwanted
homogenIsation with others. But that
changed too, with the dawn of a great idea:
Trade.

Ecce Suidae in the Vegan Hood

Dead winged pig
flying to pig heaven
you delicious bastard
you exquisite pariah
of wilderness
tell me, Pig, of those
you died for:
shapeless unicum
of chewing frenzy.

Are we worth
that wolf you ran from
would we even match
the bear that got your
grandpa at the pond?

Please report
(if yes just nod)

Many of your kind we ate
but we weren't quite done.
Your tasteless colleagues
lay on the hard shoulder
just beside the road.
They weren't worth much
never heard of squirrel
jerky, nor cured fox.
Yoked oxen we can't eat,
we'll wait till they cross.

I'm Into Veggies

I love them in a Latin, carnal way
and I like it when they meet my knife
be it à la julienne/brumoise/chiffonade.
I respect the juice burst of cherry tomatoes// fake veggies
and the awkwardness of potatoes.
Just take a chestnut mushroom or aubergine
and cut through them, tell me about their texture texture
ante litteram polystyrene prone to osmosis
NaCl *oblige*.
Veggies are great indeed but nothing compares
to frozen pizza, the vibranium shield of captain Luigi.
Broccoli already have their well-developed lore.

Brain Drain

It was not easy to accept mediocrity
or the idea of being bad sometimes
even I was a faultless plasmon eater.
I would like somebody to tell me it's not
my fault, but I don't believe in America,
and fell back on SSRIs.
Here's to a new life of involvement
and a thousand new ways to be offended;
everyone in the village has a cousin
that goes to Harvard
they will never know about the ethics
of sundried Mediterranean fishermen
→ 'cause there isn't one.

PCI

Father with l'Unità and Pasolini
tried to convince me we were good losers
but I know that not too deep inside my guts
sleeps a little fascist.
He waits there, ready to invade Albania
or Greece and proclaim a new empire
with the same face on every banknote.
He claims Argentina and Hollywood are
Italian nurseries and that there's no way
rapeseed oil is a thing.
Mother made me a good awful
catholic, but this wouldn't stop the little
bald man with the fez. He despises
buffet sushi and Harry Potter.
La vita è bella his favourite film. Sometimes
he even makes me wanna win arguments.
I need you to know my miniature Mussolini
and frankly I hope you like it, as you like my
chest hair or my toes. I want you to know
he's there when we dine out and when
your friend gets a new tattoo
and I want you to know he sleeps when you
show me your own tiny little führer

Turning Japanese

My Japanese girlfriend
stirs matcha with bamboo whisks
in her '80s Nagoya skyscraper.
She is used to earthquakes and great waves
nothing can graze her zen.
Of course she has a yukata
and wooden flip-flops
split-toe socks, sun umbrellas
and other accessories.

彼女wa always smiles with thin lips
and frets when her father's silhouette
animates the paper doors.
You don't have to, Yoko
He can't divide us now

My Japanese girlfriend has a pearl necklace
and I might even quit
as I'm done with the stirring

Eurogalactic Shield of Impenetrability

My magic bus protects me from old ladies in fur coats.
They're nice, but they voted leave.
This window seat feels like a tailor-made cockpit.
A big Bulgarian shock absorbing system to the left.
The front camera makes the road into a swift eel,
and street lights are falling stars that fade gently.
Minutes after landing I stole the job from a Ford Mondeo driver.
I couldn't get the carbon fibre bodywork.
We once raced a horse in Newmarket, me and my white
projectile

Cité Universitaire

I am lying on the springiest bed of Geneva
and my stretched arm frames you standing
you are a lit-up lava lamp
why would anybody dislike pubic hair
surely the men on the Wall wouldn't approve
but Calvinus is nothing more than a thesis title
or a white draught beer
and the Jet d'eau can't reach our sixth floor
we're in a fortress of brutalist architecture
I order Moroccan   you don't like saffron
then we watch Jaws II almost till the end

FERN BROOME RICHARDS

Fern Broome Richards is a poet based in Norwich, who has had poetry published in *Lighthouse* (Issue 10, 2016) and *Dream Forgeries* (The Winter Olympics Press, 2016), with a poetic essay, 'Against Silence', published online by Seam Editions (2017).

three morning poems

substitution cypher, without promise

    Cruel shape; tortured as a necessity
    stab it out. I said stab it out,
    it has nothing more to say.
    When there are lines on it, you know
    you have succeeded. When it is merely
    a dot, all of this is dead +
    everyone is dead in the future, I will
    <u>not</u> accept it. The song smells of bone.

    A moment without you is very outside.
    Morning burns with a cold flame, let me
    stab it out. Fire. Oh shuttle, you pass
    in cardioid arcs, I can depend on it.
    Moment of brightness. Fire. Stab it out.

    The form of telescopes of microphones
    a rumbling distant feeling, rumbling
    felt in the distance. I promise none of this
    + give you only a question of fire
    Is it snowing where you are? Is it
    on fire where you are? Moving into
    the derelict body, I saw skin ripple
    like fresh film, repeating movement
    Stab it out; it was once decent and could be
    spoken of, with this boneless thought

leave me, attend one of the many fictions
of place. o temperature, rip me up
into components that I may be reborn
as a new match. All the sulphur
of the body, all the unburnt monuments

so many measurable steps,.

allegretto

most normal item, the pork pie
split on its seams like a wounded heart
here they come——the buildings,
their distant occupants——
to dredge me once more
as an infected lake.
loving the robot is
choosing noise forever
don't worry about morning
in its functional identity to every other
scarring the one who sees it,
an image of common combat
the alchemist who flaunts his immortality
sits up in bed, says
      the asteroid!

raw rhubarb augury

when there is a future to be had   the rhubarb
growing from the wall takes on particulars
and with swift teeth bursting cells
the shape of time breaks with a crunch   soapy sour
of poison   the vapour of the green spine
haruspicy portends this   reaching into the garden
for another attempt   in the morning
boldly closed buds signify danger take a sharp
bite of fretted leaves   with sugar on
with frost the winter   demands   arms itself
acidic spikes of glass   demands   hands
the blunt knife on the   windowsill   organs
of noise   raw rhubarb in the mouth for
the coming of spring

PAUL FREDERIK CARLSEN

Paul Frederik Carlsen has lived in Germany, the UK, the USA, and Chile. He has just written a year-long collection (a poem/day). The sequence aims to be an organic and energetic exploration into his interest in relationships and intimate moments between people. The poems morph and develop throughout the work. He completed his BA in Creative Writing & Journalism at the University of Roehampton, where he graduated with first-class honours.

11th of August

if i could change anything
id not change a thing
and i love you
but its not true

you like to leave the toothpaste
open all day and night
im forced to brush my teeth
with day old crust

i love you
but i hate dry toothpaste

22nd of August

trapped by an old phone
chained to the wall
tigering up and down his
4 feet of territory

those are his
while he listens
and sighs
and gets out half sentences

if you could see him pace
his wire cage
i can see the path get worn
i can see his stripes start to show

17th of September

    sex above us
    + sex above that
    this house is filled

    in every room playful
    wet fingers
    finding their uses

    congratulations over eggs
    scrambled and salted
    together at the table

1st of November

    i dreamt of you tonight
    a vivid dream
    half erased by waking

    we did weird things

    we played golf inside
    teed off near the TV
    i almost broke the speaker
    with my swing

    but then you sat on my lap
    and i think we were happy

2nd of November

i saw you painted
and under your skin
you are green

+

i found myself in you
or maybe i didn't
it was too long ago
for me to remember

(
+

i said *i love you*
and i think i did
but see
i m blue

)

3rd of November

exploring you
your topography
as you hadn't been since
yesterday

you are your home
a long coastal line
the atacama desert

and in you
i wonder if i
am still me

21st of January

you look good in your red lipstick
since i meet you

i told you i liked red
+ you wear it when im not there

you look tanned today
at least i told you you did

(

i cant remember what your kiss
feels like

i have been trying to remember
but i wont

)

28th of January

       i saw you yesterday
       you were faster than i
       remember
       you wore the purple outfit
       with matching hat
          always a hat
       i barely caught a glimpse
       before you slipped into
       the fijian exhibition

       i waited outside
       it was cold

       you left through a
       back exit

10th of February

       when cigarettes + songs are
       inadequate measures of time
       i use beard length

       you hate my beard
       so i let it grow
       when we arent together

       right now
       i havent seen you for
       4 inches

19th of February

    id balter with you

    + fuck
    + laugh
    + drink
    + smoke

    id like to tell you it meant something
    or nothing
    just not somewhere in-between

3rd of March

        how memories work
        the piecing together
        the imagining
        the filling in

    i remember being in a basement
    in england that was in germany
    i was 4 + 3

    i remember high school
    not everyday
    definitely not every night
    i was 17–13

    i remember you
    chilean sun asado smoke
    beer + black bikini
    ██████████ + i am

5th of March

>we walked through grey bloc buildings
>\+ looked through closed doors
>we bought bleach
>\+ talked about the future

13th of March

she had a short white blonde bob cut   a designer dress   + a silver nose ring   he had no hair left   a white scruffy beard   + an old man s suit + scarf   she talked for an hour about tech/blogs/twitter/facbook/etc/   then she asked if there were any questions he said he didnt get it   the room laughed   i didnt   he didnt either   his missing-tooth-mouth closed + disappeared into his beard   i saw fear

19th of March

> daffs tricked into blooming
> by five minutes of sun
> daffs torn by gale winds
> + hail
> daffs all the way to wells-next-the-sea
> where we walked on the low-tide-exposed
> sand
> chose beach huts we liked
> + ate cod + chips
> i dont think those daffs will ever see spring

finding you
(floating poem)

> i opened a suitcase of art supplies today
> + found you in the oil pastels
> between emerald green and light blue
>
> you smelt of memory
> trapped in a small cushioned box
>
> i didn't recognise you at first
> thinking i had found you earlier
> in the faber-castell water colour pencils
>   the smell of wood
>
> but that wasn't you, was it?
> you were with the soft neopastels

DAVID CHARLES GILL

David Charles Gill writes about: the natural world; men and families; attitudes to employment. He held the 2016 Bryan Heiser Memorial Bursary and was a finalist in the Frederik van Eeden International Poetry Competition (Holland Park Press). His work has been published by *Haverthorn Magazine* and Cinnamon Press. David's first play *Nineteen Short Scenes for Sons* will be produced in Norwich next year.
davidcharlesgill.wordpress.com

I think of you a lot

        Towards the end   she lived in apple skin.

Textbooks exaggerate the Earth's crust – otherwise it would be too small to see.[1]

        Not the strong-toothed rip and perfect pop
        of parting flesh and tegument

        point three mill of polished chew
        of inter-dental parchment wedge
        the green - and red - and yell - of health

The skin to diameter ratio[2] *of a typical apple is 0.3:70 mm.*

        but skin that even being held might tear

        like tissue paper soaked to gauze
        a slipping film   on milk   her lucid bones

I think the equivalent for our planet[3] *is 25:12756 km.*

        something worn and weaker   looking in
        beyond herself - a span that's not so much
        given in   as given to   whatever waits

in rock and soil   ten thousand years.

        a mother who has tired herself   but stayed
        and stayed   to form a place grown tight with help
        and seeds   and happy wet

        her glassy world   and light breath   unsure what's in
        what's out   what's new   what's air
        what's weight   or spotted old.

Ten thousand years![4]
Ten thousand years!
Ten thousand years!

---

1 Adapted from a science blog.
2 Or 0.4% (approx.) if this helps.
3 Or 0.2% (approx.) like the thin covering on liquefying fruit.
4 Shouted. Roared. By all present.   Perhaps rehearsed.   Each roar so loud it starts to hurt.
        Each roar so sure it may bring tears.
        Each roar for anyone you may have lost.

    Text for silence. Text for one, two or more voices.

Pieta

I think you left us long ago
but cautiously   and subtly   with hidden care.

Somewhere in your early endless running summer joy
you went away.
                The children who came back each night
to eat your several meals at once were not quite you.

There was an after and before you could not join
something leaving   things left lost   and slowly too much new
a period when everything you thought would clear did not.

You slipped between our morning words
each busy suit   my knotted ties
all our inching purposes
until I came to realise
I've grieved for you for years
hoping by your side each day.

Please don't make your father clear the hair that falls across your face.
Let me   leave you.   Do not go first.

All I ever wanted   was someone who could throw a ball as well as you
who'd have a laugh and maybe chat whilst starting to love others more.

I   am   so   glad   you   are   my   son
and frightened when you cannot talk or smile.

You have seen me sit and weep and hold and kneel
and try to make you safe   keep safe   stay safe
you know too much about all that
but if you could come back to us
draw my sitting sadness here
colour me till you return
etch the hope inside your fears
compose your pain   and then come home

for we can wait   will always wait   must always wait

can't help but stay and simply wait

whilst bearing something of your weight.

August 4th

When evenings seem as close as days
we sit above the garden slope
in losing light so bats might loop
about our heads. From anywhere
their quiet air comes lower still
to somersault in orbits hung
around the giant rooves of night;
the flicker of their silent film
is near and indistinct as we
compose their half-imagined selves

From Boss Mother

(When read aloud this section is for two voices speaking the final two lines in unison)

Sexing the Boss

The day you found	your birth could come
again (again)	beside as many deaths:
between your legs	perfect needles
piercing trembling	settling in
your lower heart	your spine's soul
centred there	puncture sharp
flooding belly	breath and thought
madder button	purpled head
protuberance	fierce mouth
each mastering	the brew and burn
the grasp and shock	you think you feel
(you think and feel)	prostina deep until

    sistered into brotherness   brothered into sisterness
               you see   insist   insist   enjoy
                     declare   that you
                         are both

Dorset Stones

We brought them years ago   distorted planets in a bag.
Countenances   faintly lined with latitudes
intervals in light grey rock   their parallels oblique
suggesting atmospheres   thickened speed.

>The first
>a filled palm of smooth cold
>however held. A rounded fell
>to grip.
>
>Then twins. Quiet jupiters
>their bellies broad as paired hands
>settling anywhere.

The idea was to find some new technique
to make a painted stone look good.
They would be annotated worlds (inf.)
one for each child
to celebrate
their ways.

Till then:
together on a garage shelf
considered at the start of school
remembered every other year
unused   unnoticed   moved outside
to store their childhood stuff

dressed in dust for heat
leopards at the starts of showers
their soaking shine is seal side
marking our perimeters

                                the points at which we notice change*
                                inhabiting a given time/and given time
                                the orbit round our children's lives
composed in rain by flower beds   the purlieus of paid work perhaps
around a plate of water caught   the sought peripheries of day
for blackbirds and their young
becoming littoral
again.   go out in the height of sun   go on
                                make sure it's at its blazing heavy gorgeous best
                                spend minutes eating oranges near shade
                                face the sun and all its heat with tight skin
                                track it with your closed eyes
                                taste its sweetened energies
                                open up and drink the light
                                swallow all its oranges
                                bursting mouths of oranges
                                bright oranges   near shade
                                oranges   and shade
                                oranges   shade

a Greek view – earliest report September 2016 – Attica, the Pelepponese. Phrasal noun. Any aspect of outstanding beauty achieved by ignoring the immediate foreground. Usage includes: without maintenance, the quayside will become a Greek view; I think I'll take a Greek view on the matter; from here it looks like a bit of a Greek view.

All week there has been slaughter at our feet.
(Omitted? cropped?) the fences netting ragged flags
a swimming pool with broken walls below a harbour scene.
For little's being mended now   or tidied   cleaned
completed well   and most of what a province does
cannot be done   because the money poured away.

Of course   it's all still marvellous   in almost any light
the morning on Parnassan rocks
limestone   olives   bright bright sea
still giving us its metaphors
as brutal hill meets pure sky
as empty block or ruined bar
reminds each one to keep on looking up/beyond
and never at the twenty metres measured from our shoes.

A Greek view across the bay to Argolid. Parking
on descending roads   framing things to miss the tyres
flying bags   plastic junk   fridges and some paving stones
ancient angled monuments to what The People failed to be
and all that monetary shit   preventing us remembering
what the fuck a country's for.

30 – DAVID CHARLES GILL

From the opening of **Shit keeps getting everywhere**

You see I'm all gush me.
A fierce rabbit.
Not the silent type.
A strong verbal man more like.
Actually   not that strong
without the chance to sort things out at pace
without my daily talking cure.
Works a treat at work of course
a bit of insight   praxis   graft
plus everything belief can bring.
At home my type of help won't help
so shit keeps getting everywhere
no good for you or me.

It's taken just about a year
a weakened   broken   ruined year
to lessen all the say and do
to lose the speed in everything
whilst caring every bit as much.
Learning how to stop and wait
and wait and wait and simply be
a place for you. Learning
to do nothing. Hiding how
I truly feel by working
from the outside in
when all I really want to do
is help   and never let you go.

What used to be exceptional
(a marble on the bathroom floor
a puckered orb in rolling brown
an ageing relative's mistake
visiting a splash or smear)
has now become my finger end
or marks upon a white hem.
My daily and most unsung
skill ridiculed by cotton twill
for shit keeps getting everywhere
and will not keep its place
staying like a crumpled child who
can't be left and cannot bear to leave.

///// |||||

It took me years to learn to live with you (my fault).
Your ways keep resting by my own (each day)
I'd like us both to wipe away a stripe we made
pressing creams inside/along scored flesh
each careful split   filled   smoothed
Jesus-cured to never having been
your swollen scraping lines of cut
by cut by cut/////your blood braille
patterned like the rib/////bed sand
fingered gently/////followed often
always on the other arm
as shoulder/////badge
as raw/////flag
a red/////fence
which used to keep you in

       (soon) || the wound imposed
    by trees || which tore your side
You asked them to || *Made them*
which saw you cur||l and ||ick your mouth
your skin on theirs your softness
   barbed and he||d by puncturings
before the creasing north/south scar
      po||ished by your sun and rain
a nourished mark/marking one
one amongst your many births
a downward stroke of spear
(to dagger any word) as
purple as a pair of ||ips
which sometimes smile which
cannot make things go away

jesuscuttingjesuscuttingjesuscuttingjesuscuttingjesuscuttingjesuscuttingjesus
cuttingjesuscuttingjesuscuttingjesuscuttingjesuscuttingjesuscuttingjesuscutting

RICH LAW

Rich Law's work has appeared in *Ink, Sweat & Tears* and *Sentinel Literary Quarterly*. He was shortlisted for the 2016 Bridport Prize for Poetry. You can follow him on Twitter: @rich_lawidge

After my Funeral

It's back to work down the local
for my daughter's big scene. She's not a natural.
Last night, emptying my drawers, she wiped her eyes
on receipts. Now she's going off script again. The sole heiress
of bugger all, she's supposed to toast
her husband (a star who's never contracted
herpes) and a father-in-law who doesn't fake forgetting
birthdays.
But I'm to understand her improvised tears
contrast with cava bubbles and it's too moving
to scrap. So we raise our glasses with the last woman
I'll ever make weep. It's time to focus
on her now, her journey to forgiving herself
for forgiving me. She begins by smacking my grandson,
whose little hands still puppet her speech.
In the background I sip John Smith's with the clientele
miscast as friends and family. We pretend to talk,
but it's all for show.

Meerkat

My cookie-eyed pet. How sugary
people get admiring the Amaretti
chest and butter melted
down your legs. Who could
suspect such gentlemanly
erection and those paws
tableclothed over your
tummy? Do they not see
how quickly you're stirred
by teaspoons whispering
with cracked mugs? Tell me
what – or who – has bitten
you, my sweet.

How I Meet Your Father

I am a priest for the evening. See back then you can try your hand at different occupations. Your dad's ravishing; he confesses to talking loudly in libraries for the sexual thrill of it. He glances at me like a cat with a rat in its mouth. I already know he's never been guilty in his life. We become partners. Next morning we untie a dog from a lamppost outside a corner shop and leave it at the nearest supermarket. We get the flu before dining at posh restaurants and shining all the cutlery on our tongues. We make love on the rare occasion that we're bored. Things escalate as they will in love, which is less blind than increasingly tasteless. Looking back a train isn't the ideal vehicle to hijack. But we are so naive. The train inevitably reaches its destination, but your dad escapes out of a window.

 I am sat at a desk in the police station, waiting to be grilled, when your father walks in wearing a police uniform. We look at each other like that first time in the confessional, and I say 'get me off'. He tasers my chest, which is a metaphor that actually happens. I wake from the coma married, with two kids.

Washington Avenue Bridge

    I'd cast my trusses
    like a dreamcatcher.
    I'd bend my piers
    in prayer and dip
    their forehead lone
    into the water.
    I'd level land. Hell,
    I'd drain the river.
    But really what is here
    or there beyond
    studded reflections,
    this frozen rail,
    determined grip?

As the noose clutches a crook's neck

        stock footage appears, a loop
        of a cow fainting. Every 3 seconds
        legs lock and it topples in instant
        self-taxidermy – its eyes

        serene as glasses of milk.
        I ring the BBC helpline, tell them
        to tell this cow it's upsetting
        my niece, who tries to please but cries

        into the receiver. Automated apology.
        Programming will resume. We endure
        for 12 minutes before the cow
        starts folding onto a Union Jack.

        The Mrs puddles tea on the carpet.
        I call my MP and we agree
        this is evidently terrorism.
        The flag becomes crude

        slushy, which the cow slurps
        before puking to strains
        of La Marseillaise. I feel
        some uninvited surgeons scrape

        behind my eyes, perform
        heart surgery on the land
        of my heart and damn
        it's already in the bag.

Are you there Rich? It's me...

When I was a painter my colours overran with water. At each installation Dad would say *that clown's been crying on the fridge again*. Decades later, as the house snores and I'm snuffling about for milk & cookies, the fridge's cold stare sends in the clowns. Tonight is the tragedy of my first kiss. This consists mostly of happenings in the about-to-happen, glances passed like fingers through a Bunsen burner. I skip ahead to my friends all popcorn-eyed, cornering us on a bench. I take a moment to experience the uncanniness of a tree unchanged. Now I am her, braced, a shrivelled comet entering my atmosphere. At impact, I am alone and imagine returning to that bench tomorrow. I guess it's like sitting on set of a play you think you've seen, maybe sensing it plays out still in the space before you. A drained sky will be flooded with honking, and somebody has left the water running.

NAOMI MADLOCK

Naomi Madlock is a vegan poet who collects photographs of roadkill. At the University of Exeter, she won the Gamini Salgado prize for best dissertation by handing in a beehive filled with feminist poetry. She hopes that deploying similar gimmicks will breeze her through her Masters at UEA.

Mist

    is a gift
        given in increments
           by the wind
        to the moor

    filling your window
        to the brim

    You purchase
        a frost-laced lungful
           at the cost
        of your vision
        your horizon

        Your fingers
    dissolve before you

    All at once
        the path home
           becomes infinite
        yet footsteps away

Caesura

Celestial white noise
on the conservatory roof
as the sea draws home
a cacophony of rains.

The cat purrs torrentially
curled tight in a sofa nook
static but for a back leg that juts
out like a clock hand
ticking on the spot.

Sometimes
we need to shut up
and listen, says God
as She stomps around
in the attic.

Cyclogenesis

The crickets tick like watches wound too tight.
The cows lie down; the pond frogs rise to taste
the air that swells with expectation. I
should not be here. I fog under the weight
of a tempest in gestation. My breath
is unfamiliarly thick, and beneath
the thunder of desperate boots the earth
grows thick with worms. Folding to an early death
the path entombs itself in ferns. I throw
myself below the flora of my shawl
and falter. Nose to the grass like the cow
I am, I kneel here and upon the caw
of a birch-raised jackdaw's call to prayer
the cloud breaks and I pour and pour and pour

Refuge in the Waves

This cove is where I go to heal
white
and nude
in the salt and the moonglade
while the boats come in
   empty and upturned.

Washed inward by the waves, I return
to myself
unaware
under the spill of darkness
of others adrift here
   waterlogged, silent.

This, too, is where they came to heal
to fill their lungs at last
with air
and rinse their children's hands
of sulphurous
   dust and blood

while we washed ours
of them.
If I
am ever to bear a child
I will guide her to the water's edge
with arms as
   wide as nets.

White Bone, Grey Gold and the Void

    A distinct lack of spirits
    haunt the lake. But the owl –
            the she owl

    At badger-light I track
    the trails too slight for human feet
    in quest of her precious pellets,
        nothing before or behind in the torch beam
        nothing tangible but the stones beneath my boots
        nothing but nothing until

        her shriek
    startles the trees. I stand
    toad-still, shrew-silent,
    eyes wide as the horizon to detect
    the winking of stars in succession –
                her flightpath.

    Tawny pellets are grey thumbs
    (I'd read somewhere, or dreamt I'd read)
    dense with bone and fur   they poke
    from the litter and loam like dead men
    hitch-hiking back to the overworld.
    It is advised to keep one's eyes firmly
    planted...

    Lost in a starscape   I stumble
    on a tump of ribcage rot and plumage –

        the male
        the hoot unheard by the sky

    And she calls to him

you might think, roused by his familiar scent –
the scent of hope – kicked up from the mud
but the owl, all ear and eye, has no need
for fragrance. All eye and ear, she is, and memory.

    She cries
        He does not call back.

    She cries
        He does not call back.

He's here, I reply, as I sleeve dry one unglistening tear
    and snap
        its head from its body.

The head, at least, is salvageable,
beak intact. (Flesh too – nothing
a splash of bleach, a wad of iron wool,
won't solve.)

I scavenge sixteen pellets in total,
harvest the bones
    (femur, sternum, scapular)
in sample trays for analysis.

The owl skull
I take home for personal use.
He perches atop the desk lamp, glowing,
    glaring, eyeless and white.

At night, outside my bedroom window
when the rain subsides, and the wind,

    she cries

        He does not call back.

Look At Me Now

I have grown through your ignorance
like a tree that swallows the axe
like a housebroken tree that ruptures the roof
while you were too busy cutting my roots
to mark my branches.

I have split the corset of my juvenile bark
exposing my core, my spring of vermillion
sap adorning each scar with beads of honey
with pendants of honeyed wasps and needles
ensnared in amber.

I have seized the entire sky
in my thorned and fruit-laden hand. I am dripping
with life. Bees hang their buzzing lobes of comb
from my knuckles and nuthatches
nest in my palm.

I will never stop blossoming. Not for you.
Not for winter. I will emerge from the canopy
gulping in the light, breath pouring
from every leaf as I leave you behind
one inch at a time.

Bring Me Back as a Stone

    to begin
       with a silt-laden drop
           of water
       deep within the bowels of a cave
         where the seep of unseen substances
         may fortify my shape
to exist
    in a state of awareness
        no monk has ever mastered

and   after millennia
    after the chandeliers come crashing down
    after daylight enters the lake for the first time
       revealing its elixir of crystalline blues
    after subterranean rivers roll me on the basin
       until I am orbed and polished as a pearl
    after these rivers raise me from the well
       to bear me through a labyrinth of channels
          into the boundless open

lay me on the sand of my ancestors
    and let the tide
       draw circles round me
immobilise me
    to show what ripples may form
       from stillness
isolate me
    to teach me the breadth
       of my own beauty
silence me
    so I must learn to listen
       to the percolation of time
       as I make my granular
          return to the sea

    and   after millennia
        after the dusts of undiscovered lifeforms
            settle on the sea floor
        after the bones and shells and corals
            embrace to form one
        after the upheaval of earth
           and the transmutation
                of mineral-laden waters

bring me back as a stone

S.Z. MASON

S.Z. Mason is a poet based in Rutland, and was generously supported by The Bryan Heiser memorial bursary.

Hazmat Holiday

Memory delivered by temperature   (—hyperstitional zone)
Walking into paused rain   creating space   shadowed
Omega sunset,,   beckoning
Collecting mushrooms   (— hyperaccumulating mycorrhiza)
Throwing them into the cross-processed   sky
Because everyday is   like friday

The Empire of Light

Reborn
within their mineral sanctuary, the world controlling invisible pose as equal puppets (performing) shadow warming narrative. The ostensible option for ascent into bronze but beware of linear progression / solidity of ancient silhouettes. Phantoms are born to be allegories. Visibles must be thought vulnerable – an escape when you really are a magician. Sunlight does not reveal sincerity, it is fiction waving a false flag
the sun overcoding the stars
sky as refrain controlling illusion
by illusion. If you see the dark
then you chose the dark,.

MOLLY ELLEN PEARSON

Molly Ellen Pearson is a confessional poet from St Albans, Hertfordshire. She recieved a BA in English Literature and Creative Writing from UEA prior to her master's. She is the 2016 recipient of the Ink, Sweat & Tears Scholarship and her work has been published by Egg Box, *The Cadaverine Magazine* and the Young Poets Network.

& this, my body at night

a disused retail outlet midway to nowhere on a
hot red road leading all the way up
inside me. my open mouth is a shape that needs
to be filled. to be full. to be emptied, &
some things are better out than in. my body at night
under its parched quilt. if i close
my left eye, i can squint through its killing light
to headaches of rain, the raised voices
of clouds in an unfurnished room,
not letting it out. i used to know a girl
who vomited through windows. i asked her if
she was sick. her girl eyes said
i did not understand, that i was naive
& stupid, that i was a failure & that i did not
understand. *this*. leaning over
the threshold of yourself & sucking hard
on candy-canes of bile. if i could look down at
everything that was in me & now
isn't. if i could look back. my past, its aftertaste
proving that some things are better out
than in, but blood is not one of them. myself, touched
like a light switch with broken fingers, the sound
i am making this: *mmmnhh*. my body
at night. my body not happy unless it is
held down & forced, until chemicals with half-lives
longer than mine are bobbing in the ebb tide of
my veins. the words come only slowly but some things

are better out. when i took the drug
all i did was curl up in the nest
of its ravening silence. i could not find a noise
to put my name to.

happiness

is a nocellara olive
the last, lying back in its dish like a girl
in a green bikini basking in brine
the smell of crushed lemon
reminding me that i've never
been to sicily. even the stone is precious
nestled amongst the tender crumbs of everything
i've already been. i have always felt
so fucking entitled
for wanting. i get anxious, stuck in myself
as if the house of my face could
burn down with too much desire. anything
could happen. i could die
in a hotel room. i could die in a hotel room while
the last sweet nocellara waits outside. i could
get on a plane to sicily.
i could

suck

i like to be thin. i like the sensation of slimness, that absence,
the i of me secure in its slight frame. thin
is the barter of something for nothing, the barter of something
into nothing, a state of expection. to the touch
i'm serrated periphery, features fine
as a coin's. turned sideways, i'm barely there
& this is good. when i tried to give blood, i think
we were still together. stepping out of the clinic
i felt weightless. no recent lover of needles or queers,
those things that doctors say turn chaste veins
into sewers, foul the estuary where the heart
washes up on itself. it was just *an issue of weight*.
it makes me think of leeches, the way they suck

single-minded as if on a nipple or dick, the way
you can slit them open & milk yourself
back out. it makes me think of the way you
enclosed in your lips my bone & said *christ there is nothing of you*.
you could bite through me so cleanly. you could
bite. it makes me think how little there is
of me to give to anyone, the way
i turn sideways now & you do not see me. the i of me
unbreached in luminous isolation, cold to the touch.
the place that a leech can't bite
is the place you tried. i like to be thin. i like to be
as thin as a thing that takes, my legs
a mosquito's, my face thirsty. i like to be as thin as a thing
that will not live forever, so you don't have to imagine the bone
underneath. i cannot forget who i am, there is nothing
to shield me. i like to be thin. i like to take
off my top & my jeans with the 25 waist & stand
in front of the mirror & feel that something enormous
is squirming towards me, leechlike, end over end.

leve meaning beloved

leven lightning the act of making light

leyp what is smeared or sticks together

liep to linger or cling motions of holding

life the crease beside heart & fate

leaven what is permeated altered made to rise

lever the aspect around which others turn

leaver that which cannot be kept & now receding

leaf a thing that falls

afterward//the present becomes opaque/////i see you//////////////////////on the far side of/////////////////////////warmth especially////////////////there is////////////////my bottom drawer an instance of//////////touch between us////////////////////a polaroid that/////////////////or discloses itself like a fist////i need you to//////////////////////////////////open it///////speak////////////////////////////reflected in fixed sand we are////////////////////////////acts without purpose or meaning/////////////////& this is connection/////////////////////////tell me////////////////////am i///////////////////////////////or am i a////////////////need that walks downstairs in the dark////////////////fearful & thirsty/////i say////////////////////open it////////////////////eyes///the pursed shrunk heart of my///////////////////////////mouth &/////////////sucked you off////////////you couldn't stand to///////////////open it/////////////////////////that sense of receding like////////repeating a strange word until////////////////////meaning occurs in///////////////////////////////every gap you might walk//////////////past any shard where there///////////////////is a chance of////////seeing you

everfixer

fourth cycle of year   white in the trees   that time
when everything starts to move closer   faster
open out   & i don't know who to be   except
back to the same
    vast institutes of sunshine
their warmth apparatus   alongside the realisation
that i have forgotten   how to be touched   how even to
want to be
this body   a murmuration   drunk in the day
    the sunlight   breaking
into component parts

JAKE REYNOLDS

Jake Reynolds was born and raised in Lincoln, and in 2015 was long-listed for the National Poetry Competition. In 2016, he was awarded UEA's Malcolm Bradbury Prize for his undergraduate dissertation. His poetry has appeared in *HVTN*, *The Cadaverine Magazine*, *A Tale of Four Cities*, and on BBC Radio 3. In 2017, Seam Editions published his creative-critical project 'Left Alone'. He tweets @JakeAReynolds.

Frozen Aisle

In amongst weird nuggets and chunks
I find a fillet of lightly dusted bream
but like an italicised cartoon heart
this is useless to me

further down
sloping like an indoor pool

all these potential feasts
lying in the dark

you can freeze just about anything
knowing you'll forget it's there:

hotel door keys, gift ribbons, tea cosies
and letters
which in particular take on a historical quality
when frozen

all the dead bits pulped and mashed
into the shapes of longer-dead things
the turkey pterodactyl
pollock troglodyte
and scampi
the veiny shrapnel
of whatever got us here

people bring their own

on more than one occasion I have seen
a person lay a cocoon of blankets
down into the chests of frost
each fleece or sheet imprinted
with stars, ringed planets, and other cold things of the universe

Shona Beverley's Five Mantras for the Self-Effacing Widow

<u>1</u>

Grief, grief, grief. Take your hand in mine and we'll form a circle.
O grief! That we could banish you, O! Louder, louder!
Grief! Good god! Slithering round my kimono! Out!

<u>2</u>

Widow is an odd word and I urge you all
to reconsider its connotations, to forget
the spider and mournful 'oh'. Today
let's think about *windows*. You know what
they say. Let's get some air in.

<u>3</u>

Since our meetings start at noon
we do not serve red wine.
In fact let's all urge each other not to fall
into that blood-leak panacea, staining our teeth
with loss. Say, *I am slow-roasted coffee.*
I am worth time. I am worth the toll it takes.

<u>4</u>

I am sorry.	*I am sorry.*
I am not sorry.	*I am not sorry.*
There are some things	*There are some things*
I cannot control.	*I cannot control.*
Some things I lose.	*Some things…*
Some things I gain each day.	*…I lose, some things I…*

<u>5</u>

It's okay to expect to see him in places
he often visited when alive, we were all
young women once parading round town
saying we would never need a man
and that's true, we never did, that's true,
we never do, that's true, still true.

Dramatic Presentation of the Fireside Tradition

[flourish]

Swept away by a raptor's breath,
we are all good stories.

[flourish]

THIS
    was all once a fireside story which began in the grizzle
    and spit of faces which begrudged the cinder platforms
    rising into the canopy and leaving small, scorched gifts.

NOW
    an adolescent gathering tries to forge fire with two-stick
    friction until a baby flame blooms from the black and
    all boom and clap backs and blush like hot ash.

    The glow from a rogue smoulder slips up
    leaving no trace, looking for old friends
    to gather in new places.

THESE
    new places are votive tablets alive and spinning with an
    electric once reserved for nervous systems and synapses
    like birds skating Os overhead, once reserved for love.

HERE
    they are, the good stories now constituting the grizzle
    and spit, each a new beauty alone evading death,
    each a new institution, swept away by hot breath:

[darkness]

I fell asleep because I suck   I don't do early nights I just like being in bed I enjoyed tonight   I suck at self-love

send pics   I befriended a toddler today   I gave her chips I am so inhospitable   send pics   my hair smells of smoke

sorry I didn't reply I'm cooking a Thai green curry   send pics you can borrow one of mine   I destroy everything   did you come home in the end?   we should have toasted marshmallows on sticks   I am ravenous   just did a quiz to find out what pizza I'd be

am I annoying you   do you think you're monkish   I hate being lied to   I feel truly earthly   I feel like an earthling

say something brutal   I like the ugly truth   I get you send pics   you should hate me   amaze me

[darkness still]

you should hate me   amaze me

/

First Light
For Jim

> Safety-blanket morning treats us
> to duckling clouds and tufts
> waking over tiers of spruce.
> The sun powders the earth
> yellow with its warm-up scent.
>
> It's like no harm has come
> to anything, not ever.
> Pluming, breaths make a point.
> Alive alive in the house of what's left.
> Alive alive in pavonine music.
> Alive alive oh. Listen and stay close.
>
> Hours after your death my nose started bleeding.
> It ran down and made my teeth stark with red.
> It tasted vital. The four of us lit a candle.

Tom in Love

here he is!   sick-skipping his merry way to the taxi rank in a floral shirt
looking like a panel show comic   our old friend, Tom.

It must have been three years   he stopped using hair gel when he saw
his friends return to him   sporting remarkable hairstyles

it feels right to cheer him on   champion him   here he is! rolling
his forehead against the toilet bowl   even if the sting of his
ringing phone does wake his mother, no matter   they are all each other
has got

here is Tom laughing   marvelling at his gutmachine   the intricate
pumps of his insides   and the brilliant fluorescent gush of the night
leaving him   to return to the pipes and filters that have kept him warm

our particularly underrated   and slightly broken friend, Tom. Our friend
giddy with charge   when Shona is woken and bangs on the door

our gently underweight friend   dancing in a rictus of the evening's loss
looking down at his phone   hearing the kettle downstairs
roll to a boil   keeping everything from everyone   most of all himself,

Tom. Who like a child wants to be emptied of his nightmares and returned
to himself   who wants to shout   I'm in love I'm in love! because he can

our friend   drunk and we allow him this moment
to make ourselves feel better   really we know that the phone might
be pizza he forgot he ordered   or a friend who has taken his coat
but   hypnotised by the pendulum   of his descending ribbon of bile,

Tom thinks   oh fuck it   things are looking up

OLIVIA WALWYN

Olivia Walwyn was born in 1983. She has worked as a school librarian, and has also competed internationally as a cross-country, mountain and road runner. Her poems have been published in *The Rialto*, *The North*, *Ariadne's Thread*, *Agenda*, *Orbis*, *The Seventh Quarry*, *Ink* magazine, and on The Poetry Society website.

Moorland Fell Run

Once you've hared it
along the opening path
furrowed with stones –
an old farmer's track

swerving from right
to left for balance
along leaping tongues
of perilous grass

and rounded the terrace
that borders the gill,
feet aligned
like you balance a beam

once you've gained open ground
found yourself in a gap
strung like loose beads
ascending, on task

and brushing the hill
like lace against skin
that dances, not stills
to the jiggling beck

of bright moving people
like streamers on masts –
a royal regatta
sailing, in gasps

of cool moorland air
that blow you off kilter
or funnel you up
in a vague helter-skelter

your shins leaning in
with bare yellow wisps
sprung from the soil
and lighting the mist

so you're tripping, in paces
that borrow the breeze
like treading a bubble
that rolls under feet

once the hill gets more steep
and you slow to a plod
working the triceps
and grinding the trod

that scuffs over boulders
and ramblingly winds
through narrow passages
gaining the heights

once you've spotted your neighbour
and kept him in sight
as the clouds build and gather
until soon, you find

he's the one bit of shine
that holds you on course
as you bound over bog,
heather bouncing you back

and sides giving way
as you slither down slopes
and clamber up gullies
that hide in the gloam

while you rise and you rise
like a prow in the waves
that ploughs through a storm
finds a route, finds a way

to be all but lost
to all but the moor,
the search for that step,
the stagger and fall

of each breath that floats
on the droplets around
the space you inhabit,
the vastness of sound

the calm and the quiet
the stillness inside
you carry home with you
– a runner for life.

Prayer

May this always be; this char
of birdsong in the trees,
this lighting of the poplars, dusk

making a silver stream
of the muddy path. That
sudden ruffle of a moorhen's

plash; this tangle of seed, tuft
of a jacket's tear. A train hoots.
Cars sigh like an ocean

full in for evening – a tide
that's abandoned the moon's pull.
May it always be kept

lapping at the edge
while we stand here, this solitude.
The sky's white, ensnared

in the river, drained of everything
until it is sure of what it has:
these reeds, this sound

absolved in dark, this land.

Rain on two sides of this room
and the birds singing through it.

       It comes over you, like dawn does
       over the marshes, even in the rain.
       Through the rain, and I think
       of the time, in a coach travelling
       over butter-brown fields I decided
       to confront something else, and often
       when you look at feelings in the face
       they just disappear, or when you
       smile for instance, just change
       the way you want the world to look
       it does, it seems to run into
       the channels of your face and then
       get blinked away, like rain, like rain.

Tonight

we go down to the pier
and pause half way along, just as
an eddy of water might swerve

back on itself, at the tide's turn.
It's then you ask me how I know
when to turn, when the walk's done

(you always continue until
you've walked round the perimeter)
I falter there, unused

to being the one who makes such
decisions, and in that space
hear where it would be – if one

came here alone. Lead the way
to the side, and we both look out
into the black beyond the rail

listening for the edge of water –
where it comes and laps against
the brim of my ear, like a shell

in the damp sand; I try to explain

Kingfisher

River held in the cliffbank
oh, and water gargling like it was
cupped to someone's mouth

River teased to the surface
flattered by the sky

I did not write anything
just there in the river's shiver

And then a line, a line
of electric blue

I followed it, slowly, slower,
stealthily as frost

over the Japanese gardens
and the deltas, and I looked
into the branches
till that chest showed

russet, hidden,
as long as I would stay.

A fox came.
A woodpecker's creaking door

opened a slant of light
across the valley.

ARRON WESTBROOK

Arron Westbrook is a poet, journalist, and content writer from Hull. His work has been featured in various print and web outlets.

Fragments from I live here, too

    in the first place *we don't like* is the first
    movement towards 'blob' – sell us
    a new sort of total but not the one that's
    value cornflakes soaked in cold water
    or one that's best in best of both

i love you niacin b3 thiamin b1
fedex me $C_6H_{10}CaO_4$ to stop the rot
for i just can't help love that this loaf
will outlive the cave that they've put

us in the credits

```
$               $                $
        $              $                 $
$$              $                $
        $              $                 $         $
$               $                $
        $              $                 $         $
$               $                $
        $              $                 $         $
$               $                $
        $              $                 $         $
$               $                $
        $              $                 $         $
$               $                $
        $              $                 $         $
```

something dropped from the sky like hail

they looked like snowflakes

plagued through letterboxes

thought they were grasshoppers

taxonomically speaking locusts and grasshoppers are the same

with a high-density destructive personality

they are considered locusts

white glistening cloud of destruction

the people had already withered

in the 1873 economic panic

200million insectobombs

came thereafter[1]

---

[1] Favourite foods are plants in the grass family such as corn, wheat, barley and alfalfa. They aren't picky, however, and can eat many other types of ∞

8

i sometimes wonder
which is closer to powder
leonard's fruit or
billie holliday

a shop soiled french stick
stolen from Tesco
snapped in half
i stitched back together
with the brightest red thread
after a few months tied to
blackening steak rind
it was nothing but dust

i became obsessed with string
tying the legs of the coffee table
to the lattices of the flat pack
laundry basket
the dining room chairs
to the broken tap
complete integration

i was trapped
i couldn't move without falling

E.F. WILLIS

E.F Willis read English at the University of York, where she co-founded *The Narrator*. She was published by Café Writers, winning the Norfolk Prize in 2016's competition and reads regularly at events. Originally from Stockton-on-Tees, her work reflects post-industrial landscapes and the body's relation to urban space. She is passionate about changing attitudes to disability through writing. Find her at www.emilywillisblog.wordpress.com.

Loops, Trimdon Wood

From the field they regard us
moon eyes steaming
I want to break
their vigil but watching
my breath amass
keeps speech back

you know
where to step
slipping past
the fish-rippled pools
but I am slapped
back by twigs
for inappropriate shoes
and lifting me like this is
ambitious

she pelts after them
all ears and tongue
her muscles are punishing
juddering but
there is none of their lashes
their silence about her
antlers only branches
flitting further
between
November light

We stream
limbs and pink cheeks
along the surface
is it odd for you
to look into this hole
to see yourself in ice? I felt
its fingers pushing back pushing up
clawing for light
and think of being
swallowed by soil
in its gut of being gutted by soil
swallowing it

the pines have flung themselves
over and over the old path
your reaching is lost
in branches I press my toes
into the shape of heels
we walk over and over the path
rooted in movement your reaching
is lost
we pull bits of mine out of the heap
needled between stumps and roots
finger the ridges of conveyors
and think of this ending up
in some crafted photo
become a museum of itself
day runs salmon grey down the edge of the stile
     just as I will pool these scraps of you
for however long we have to touch them

Photos Untaken

[a number of oranges unspecified flipping the sky on its back

[drip dry skies not quite
seal but half grey   like steel

[distant blackness comes steeled back to life it could be any light   head lamps nodding at bends   the arcade painting promises   emergency exits   cigarette pitched too soon

[*pitch now*
over the railings   blue of something you wouldn't eat
onto sand   or rock
will only know on impact

[tyre tracks impact the sand   vertical   they break off at the waves

[the breakers they break
us in sound
we can't see

[sea flickers   syncing ships in a silent rave

[he speaks at length about the ravenous   defensive floods   and tides
that grate their tongues over bodies dredging thorns to the edge of paws

[prints pause
part way along the dune

[listen   at night the dunes softly unwind

[my biting fingers unwinding in your mouth when you cast yourself around when this urge to freeze you is endless but isn't when you say this doesn't work in low resolution

[something is resolved in the oil drum   incited to flame

Rheumatology

— the study of rooms
rooms that are waiting for distances

between themselves and the things inside. I
wait for the last appointment and stare at the vent

cobwebbed where light is spun out between breaths.
A figure appears in the corridor stirring reluctant bulbs.

I study him. He seems to have been out on the tarmac
slipperless dragging a mercurial mechanism.

Feet crack under the pressure of stepping between
air and composite vinyl. He wants to become room off

white but sits and says something like a name. He waits
becoming slower becoming still. I read into the stillness

her life the life of this name
how she loved the way she walked

      Something is pulling her out of me running
into the end of a Gus Van Sant

where still the roads somehow more remote
still the characters somehow not

Dinosaur Plasters

bus   little finger splinter little dinosaur   bus   a man reprints a picture adding to his flattened image   bus   yoga yoga yoga yoga the mat keeps curling up around my feet   bus   jogger feeling the shape of muscles torn   bus   *c-y-c-l-i-s-t*/bus   hauling up her eight-months-gone woman gives her seat to someone swaying   bus   people are writing on carriage doors   bus   licking permanent markers   bus   bus   spitting into glass   bus   bus   bus   someone lies down in the road and refuses to move   bus   bus   bus   bus   bus   bus bus busbusbusbusbusbusbusbusbusbusbusbusbusbusbus

Breast Lump

I dreamed you were dead. Or I was
    wearing an old pair of trousers
down the garden attacking the hedge.
It was so aggressively alive, so hopelessly
green, spitting edges at me and everywhere
in splitting lines, white sticky hearts of leylandii
was your name.

ACKNOWLEDGEMENTS

Thanks are due to the School of Literature, Drama and Creative Writing at UEA in partnership with Egg Box Publishing for making the UEA MA Creative Writing anthologies possible.

We'd also like to thank the following people:
Tiffany Atkinson, Trezza Azzopardi, Stephen Benson, Scott Brown, Clare Connors, Andrew Cowan, Giles Foden, Rachel Hore, Kathryn Hughes, Thomas Karshan, Peter Kitson, Philip Langeskov, Timothy Lawrence, Jean McNeil, Paul Mills, Jeremy Noel-Tod, Denise Riley, Lisa Robertson, Sophie Robinson, Helen Smith, Rebecca Stott, Henry Sutton, George Szirtes, Matt Taunton, Ian Thomson, Steve Waters, Julia Webb, Peter Womack

Nathan Hamilton at UEA Publishing Project, and Emily Benton.

Editorial team: Paul Carlsen, Fearghal Hall, Margaret Hedderman, Helen James, Andrew Kenrick, Sally Shippam, Sofie Solbø, Andrew Turner, George Utton, Emily Willis, Alexa Lim Xiangyin.

UEA Creative Writing MA Anthology: Poetry, 2017

First published by Egg Box Publishing, 2017
part of UEA Publishing Project Ltd.

International © 2017 retained by individual authors.

Cover image by Caro Woods, 2014. From the collection
'My Nativity, a Soupy Opera'. Found at carowoods.com

This book is sold subject to the condition that it shall not, by way of trade or otherwise, be lent, resold, hired out, stored in a retrieval system, or otherwise circulated without the publisher's prior consent in any form of binding or cover other than that in which it is published and without a similar condition including this condition being imposed on the subsequent purchaser.

A CIP record for this book is available from the British Library.
Printed and bound in the UK by Imprint Digital.

Designed by Emily Benton.
emilybentonbookdesigner.co.uk

Proofread by Sarah Gooderson.
Distributed by NBN International
10 Thornbury Road Plymouth
PL6 7PPT +44 (0)1752 2023102
e.cservs@nbninternational.com

ISBN: 978-1-911343-24-0